The Water Mu

by

George Frederic Handel

Water parties were numerous enough during the 18th century, and surely none was more attractive to eye and ear than that of the " Royal progress " of King George the First, with " Musick by Mr. Hendel," which event took place on the River Thames, 17th July, 1717.   On Friday of the same week the " Daily Courant " comments : —

" On Wednesday evening at about 8, the King took water at Whitehall in an open barge, wherein were also the dutchess of Bolton, the dutchess of Newcastle, the Countess of Godolphin, Madam Kilmanseck, and the Earl of Orkney, and went up the river towards Chelsea.

Many other barges with persons of quality attended, and so great a number of boats, that the whole river in a manner was covered: a city company's barge was employed for the musick, wherein were fifty instruments of all sorts, who play'd all the way from Lambeth, the finest symphonies, composed express for this occasion, by Mr. Hendel: which His Majesty liked so well, that he caused it to be play'd over three times in going and returning."

Handel composed the WATER MUSIC about 1715, but the existence of the complete autograph manuscript is doubtful.   John Walsh, of Catherine Street, Strand, published an edition of the Instrumental parts about 1732, described as " The Celebrated Water Musick in seven Parts via. Two FRENCH HORNS Two VIOLINS or HOBOYS a Tenor and a Thorough Bafs for the HARPSICORD or BASS VIOLIN " and consisting of nine sets of pieces, twenty-one movements in all.

Some years later, probably 1743, the same publisher issued a " Compleat " edition for Harpsicord, with extra sets of music, a total of forty-one movements.   So popular became Handel's " WATER MUSICK " that to some of the tunes words were added, and this during the composer's life time.   " Phyllis the lovely, the charming, the fair " being an example that appeared attached to a Minuet.· History repeats itself to this day, but at least we wait until the composer is no longer with us and has become " classical."

The River Thames continues to flow, and the music of Handel still delights, but Thames water parties now-a-days are not what they were in King George the First's reign.   Although we cannot visualise the 18th century water party, we can, by way of the pianoforte arrangement of Granville Bantock, enjoy the music.

George Frederic Handel was born on 23rd February, 1685, at Halle, Lower Saxony, the son of a barber-surgeon. He received his first music lessons from Friedrich Wilhelm Zachau (1663-1712), composer, theorist and organist.   At the age of 17, he entered Halle University as a law student, but soon left for Hamburg, where he played violin in the opera theatre orchestra.   At the age of 20 Handel produced "Almira,' and in 1706 visited Italy.   Later he returned to Germany, but soon left for England, where he remained for the rest of his life, apart from a few short visits to his native Saxony.

Handel composed an astonishing amount of music of endless variety—instrumental music, operas, oratorios and lesser works, very often written at high speed.   Some few years before his death the composer became blind, and just before he died, while so afflicted, conducted a performance of the " Messiah " at Covent Garden.   Handel died in London, 14th April, 1759, and six days afterwards was buried in Poets' Corner, Westminster Abbey.   Some three thousand people attended the last ceremony in the Abbey, a tribute to the man and his genius.

HERBERT C. PERCY.

THE
WATER MUSICK
of
GEORGE FREDERIC HANDEL
ARRANGED FOR PIANOFORTE BY
GRANVILLE BANTOCK

•

Contents

PAXTON MUSIC

Order No: NOV 915674

Overture

1

SEGUE

2

3

Adagio e staccato

4

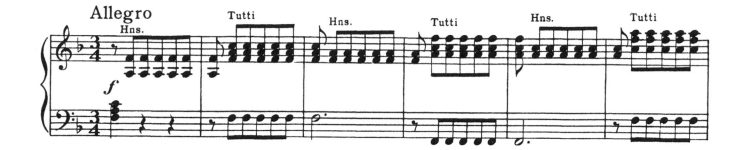

5

6

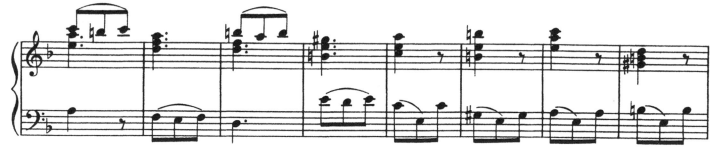

7

Air

FINE

8

Trio

9

3 times {
1st time Violins
2nd ″ Oboes
3rd ″ Tutti
}

Bourrée

10

Hornpipe

FINE

11

Allegro

12

Pomposo

14

15

FINE

Minor

D.C.

16

17

18

19

20 (a)

20 (b)

21